▌ Know my debugging toolkit.

before:
I want to know $THING but I don't know how to find out.

now:
I KNOW! I'll use tcpdump!

▌ most importantly: I learned to like it!

before: oh no a bug

now: I think I'm about to learn something!

↳ facial expression: determination.

{what you'll learn}

I can't teach you in 20 pages to ♡ debugging. (though I'll try anyway!) I can show you some of my {debugging toolkit} though!

These are the tools I reach for when I have a question about a program I want to know the answer to. By the end of this zine, I hope to have given you a few new tools to use!

section 1: I/O and ★ system calls ★

In this zine, there are 3 sections of tools that I love.

For each tool, I'll tell you why it's useful and give an example. Each one is either:

{LINUX ONLY} or {OS X too!}

Some of the most basic questions you might have when you log into a misbehaving machine are:

- is this machine writing to or reading from disk? The network?
- are the programs reading files? Which files?

So, we're starting with finding out which resources are being used and what our programs are doing.
Let's go!

dstat

I love dstat because it's
<u>super simple</u>. Every second, it
prints out how many bytes were
written to the network/disk that second.

Once, I had an intermittently slow database
server. I opened up dstat and stared at the
output while monitoring database speed.

```
$ dstat
```

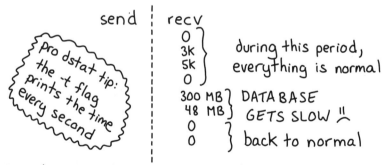

```
          send ┊ recv
               ┊  0  ⎫
               ┊  3k ⎬  during this period,
               ┊  5k ⎭  everything is normal
               ┊  0
               ┊ 300 MB ⎫ DATABASE
               ┊  48 MB ⎭ GETS SLOW ‼
               ┊  0  ⎫
               ┊  0  ⎬  back to normal
```

Pro dstat tip: the -t flag prints the time every second

Could 300 MB coming in over the
network mean... a 300 MB database query?

⋛ YES! ⋚

This was an AWESOME CLUE that
helped me isolate the problem query.

! {strace} !

LINUX ONLY

strace is my favorite program. It prints every system call your program used. It's a cool way to get an overall picture of what your program is doing, and I ♡ using it to answer questions like "which files are being opened?"

```
$ strace python my_program.py
```

read a file!
```
open("/home/bork/.config_file) = 3
read(3, "the contents of the file")
      ... hundreds of lines ...
```
← file descriptor

networking!
```
connect(5, "172.217.0.163")
sendto(5, "hi!!!")
```
↖ send "hi!!!"
← to 172.217.0.163

 WARNING strace can make your programs run 50x slower. Don't run it on your production database!

I can't do justice to strace here, but I have a whole other zine about it at:

wizardzines.com

opensnoop !
eBPF !

{OS X too! (kind of)}

When you run

```
$ opensnoop -p PID
```

it will print out {in real time} every file being opened by a program. You might think...

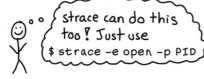

{strace can do this too! Just use
```
$ strace -e open -p PID
```
}

... and you would be right. But strace can make your program run 50x slower. opensnoop won't slow you down.

≡ how to get it ≡

Requires: Ubuntu 16.04+ or a ~ 4.14+ kernel version

Installation instructions at:

github.com/iovisor/bcc

{there are lots of eBPF powered tools! Check out that GitHub repo to learn more!}

≡ how it works ≡

opensnoop is a script that uses a new kernel feature called ⋅eBPF⋅. eBPF is fast!

There's also an opensnoop on OSX & BSD! That one is powered by dtrace.

section 2: networking

I've devoted a lot of space in this zine to networking tools, and I want to explain why.

A lot of the programs I work with communicate over HTTP.

request

"GET /cats /42" => | my program | => { name: "frufru" color : "blue" }

response

Every programming language uses the same network protocols! So the network is a nice language-independent place to answer questions like:

* was the request wrong, or was it the response?
* is my service even running?
* my program is slow. Whose fault is that?

Let's go!

netcat

handcrafted artisanal networking

HTTP requests are just text, and you can use netcat to make any HTTP request you want by hand.
Here's how to make a request for example.com! Try it!

```
printf "GET / HTTP/1.1\r\nHost:
        example.com\r\n\r\n"
| nc example.com 80
```

You should get a response back with a bunch of HTML!
You can also use netcat to send huge files over a local network quickly:

step 1: (on target machine)
```
$ hostname -I *
192.168.2.132
$ nc -l 9931 > bigfile
```
this listens on the port!

step 2: (on the source)
```
cat bigfile |
  nc 192.168.2.132 9931
```
this sends the data!

★ you can also use ifconfig to get your IP address

★ netstat ★ ⟨LINUX ONLY⟩

Every network request gets sent to a
<u>port</u> (like 80) on a computer. To
receive a request, a program (aka "server")
needs to be "listening" on the port. Finding
out which programs are listening on which
ports is really easy. It's just:

★ tuna, please! ★

also known as

```
$ sudo netstat -tunapl
```

Here's what you'll see:

```
proto    local address   PID / program name
 tcp       0.0.0.0:8080   2993 / python
              ↖port
```

So! I ♡ netstat because
it tells me which processes
are using which ports.

On OSX, use ⌐lsof -Pni⌐ instead

♡ ngrep ♡

{OS X too!}

{grep your network!}

ngrep is my favorite starter network spy tool! Try it right now! Run:

```
sudo ngrep -d any metafilter
```

Then go to http://metafilter.com in your browser. You should see matching network packets in ngrep's output! We are SPIES! ☺

Once at work, I made a change to a client so that it sent

{"some_id": ...}

with all its requests. I wanted to make sure it was working, so I ran:

```
sudo ngrep some_id
```

I found out everything was okay. ☺

{OS X too!} ⌣ tcpdump ⌣

tcpdump is the most difficult
networking tool we'll discuss
here, and it took me a
while to ♡ it. I use it to
save network traffic to analyze later!

> see
> wizardzines.com
> for a zine
> all about
> tcpdump!

```
sudo tcpdump port 8997
   -w service.pcap
```

> ❗ a pcap file ("packet capture") is the standard for saving network traffic. Everything understands pcap. ♥

> ❗ port 8997 is actually a tiny program in the Berkeley Packet Filter (BPF) language. These programs are compiled and they run really fast!

Some situations where I'll use tcpdump:

★ I'm sending a request to a machine and I want to know where it's even getting there. tcpdump port 80 prints every packet on port 80.

★ I have some slow network connections and I want to know whether to blame the client or server (also need wireshark!)

★ I just want to print out packets to see them. (tcpdump -A)

Wireshark

Wireshark is an {amazing} GUI tool for network analysis. Here's an exercise to learn it! Run this:

```
$ sudo tcpdump port 80 -w http.pcap
```

While that's running, open metafilter.com in your browser. Then press Ctrl+C to stop tcpdump. Now we have a pcap file to analyze!

```
$ wireshark http.pcap
```

Explore the Wireshark interface! Questions you can try to answer:

① What HTTP headers did your browser send to metafilter.com?

    (hint: search `frame contains "GET"`)

② How long did the longest request take?

    (hint: click Statistics → Conversations)

③ How many packets were sent to metafilter.com's servers?   replace with metafilter.com's IP

    (hint: search `ip.dst == 54.186.13.33`)

section 3 : CPU + {perf}

Your programs spend a lot of time on the CPU! Billions of cycles. What are they DOING?!

This section is about using {perf} to answer that question. perf is a Linux-only tool that is extremely useful and not as well known as it should be.

Some things I didn't have space for in this section but wanted to mention anyway:

* ★ valgrind
* ★ the Java ecosystem's fantastic tools (jstack, Visual VM, Yourkit), which your language is probably jealous of
* ★ ftrace (for linux kernel tracing)
* ★ LTTng (ditto)
* ★ eBPF

♡ perf ♡

perf is not simple or elegant. It's a weird multitool that does a few different, very useful things. First, it's a ⎡sampling profiler⎤

Try running:

$ sudo perf record python *(saves a file perf.data)*
(press Ctrl+C after a few seconds)

You can look at the results with:

$ sudo perf report

Mine says it spent 5% of its time in the PyDict_GetItem function. Cool! We learned a tiny thing about the CPython interpreter.

Shows you C functions

if you use perf to profile a Python program, it'll show you the C functions (symbols) from the CPython interpreter, not the Python functions.

Works everywhere ♡

perf can be installed on pretty much any Linux machine. The exact features it has will depend on your kernel version!

perf is for everyone

One day, I had a server that was using 100% of its CPU. Within about 60 seconds, I knew it was doing regular expression matching in Ruby. How? perf top is like top, but for <u>functions</u> instead of <u>programs</u>.

$ sudo perf top

process	PID	%	function
ruby	1957	77	match_at

perf top doesn't always help. But it's easy to try, and sometimes I learn something!

Ruby's internal regexp matching function!

... especially for Java and node devs!

Remember when I said perf only knows C functions? It's not quite true. node.js and the JVM (Java, Scala, Clojure) have both taught perf about their functions.

≡ node ≡

Use the -- perf-basic-prof command line option

≡ Java ≡

Look up perf-map-agent on GitHub and follow the directions

flamegraphs

Flamegraphs are an *awesome* way to visualize CPU performance. Generate them with Brendan Gregg's flamegraph.pl tool:

≥ github.com/brendangregg/flamegraph ≤

Here's what they look like:

eat 10%		bite 20%		teeth 28%
panda 20%		alligator 80%		
main 100%				

They're constructed from collections (usually thousands) of stack traces sampled from a program. The one above means 80% of the stack traces started with $\begin{bmatrix} \text{main} \\ \text{alligator} \end{bmatrix}$ and 10% with $\begin{bmatrix} \text{main} \\ \text{panda} \\ \text{eat} \end{bmatrix}$.

You can construct them from perf recordings (see Brendan Gregg's flamegraph GitHub for how), but lots of other unrelated tools can produce them too. I ♡ them.

Spy on your CPU!

Your CPU has a small cache on it (the L1 cache) that it can access in ~0.5 nanoseconds!  200 times faster than RAM!

tip! google "Latency numbers every programmer should know!"

If you're trying to do an operation in microseconds, CPU cache use matters!

how do I know if my program is using those caches?

perf stat!

tip
pass -e to request a specific statistic

| how to use it |
$ perf stat ls

This runs ls and prints a report at the end

| how it works |
Your CPU can track all <u>kinds</u> of counters about what it's doing. perf stat asks it to count things (like L1 cache misses) & report the results.

 Hardware is <u>cool</u>. I've never used perf stat in earnest, but I think it's awesome that you can get so much info from your CPU!